My GOVERNMENT

Standing in the Secretary of State's Shoes

Caitie McAneney

Cavendish Square

New York

Published in 2016 by Cavendish Square Publishing, LLC
243 5th Avenue, Suite 136, New York, NY 10016

Copyright © 2016 by Cavendish Square Publishing, LLC

First Edition

Website: cavendishsq.com

This publication represents the opinions and views of the author based on his or her personal experience, knowledge, and research. The information in this book serves as a general guide only. The author and publisher have used their best efforts in preparing this book and disclaim liability rising directly or indirectly from the use and application of this book.

CPSIA Compliance Information: Batch #WS15CSQ

All websites were available and accurate when this book was sent to press.

Library of Congress Cataloging-in-Publication Data

McAneney, Caitie.
Standing in the secretary of state's shoes / by Caitie McAneney.
p. cm. — (My government)
Includes index.
ISBN 978-1-50260-467-5 (hardcover) ISBN 978-1-50260-466-8 (paperback)
ISBN 978-1-50260-468-2 (ebook)
1. United States. — Department of State — Juvenile literature.
2. United States — Foreign relations administration — Juvenile literature. I. McAneney, Caitie. II. Title.
JZ1480.M34 2016
327.73—d23

Editorial Director: David McNamara
Editor: Amy Hayes
Copy Editor: Cynthia Roby
Art Director: Jeffrey Talbot
Designer: Alan Sliwinski
Senior Production Manager: Jennifer Ryder-Talbot
Production Editor: Renni Johnson
Photo Research: J8 Media

The photographs in this book are used by permission and through the courtesy of: Christopher Boswell/Shutterstock.com, cover; Sean Gallup/Getty Images, 4; AgnosticPreachersKid/File:U.S. State Department - Truman Building.JPG/Wikimedia Commons, 6; Cem Ozdel/Anadolu Agency/Getty Images, 8; Pornchai Kittwongsakul/AFP/Getty Images, 9; Sean Gallup/Getty Images, 10; Evan Vucci/AFP/Getty Images, 12; Brendan Smialowski/AFP/Getty Images, 14; Joe Cavaretta/Sun Sentinel/MCT/Getty Images, 17; Mandel Ngan/AFP/Getty Images, 18; Alex Wong/Getty Images, 20; J. David Ake/AFP/Getty Images, 21; Chris Maddaloni/CQ Roll Call/Getty Images, 23; Andresr/Shutterstock.com, 24; © BrokenSphere/Wikimedia Commons/File:Redwood City City Hall entrance 1.JPG/Wikimedia Commons, 26; Dr Ajay Kumar Singh/Shutterstock.com, 27; Monkeybusinessimages/iStock/Thinkstock, 28.

Printed in the United States of America

TABLE OF CONTENTS

John Kerry became secretary of state on February 1, 2013.

Our government has many **officials** who work to keep American **citizens** safe. One such official is the secretary of state.

There are three branches to the US government: legislative, executive, and judicial. The executive branch carries out laws, and its head is the president. A group of officials called the cabinet help the president. The highest-ranking official in the cabinet is the secretary of state. The secretary of state handles **foreign** matters, including our **relationships** with other countries. The secretary of state also works to keep peace. This protects us, or keeps us safe, from unnecessary wars and loss of human rights.

The Harry S. Truman building in Washington, DC, has been home to the Department of State since the late 1940s.

CHAPTER ONE

The Responsibilities of the Secretary of State

The US secretary of state is a busy person and has many responsibilities, or duties. The secretary is in charge of the Department of State. The US Department of State is responsible for all foreign, or international, relations of the United States. The department, as well as the position of secretary of state, was created in 1789.

The Department of State works to offer diplomacy to other countries. Diplomacy is the act of handling situations between nations in a peaceful way. The US Department of State is based in the Harry S. Truman Building in Washington, DC, which is close to the White House.

Hillary Clinton, a former secretary of state, shakes hands with the secretary-general of the United Nations.

The secretary of state is a very important person. He or she **advises** the president of the United States about foreign policy. Foreign policy is the way a government works with other nations. The secretary of state also advises the president on who should be named as diplomatic **representatives**, such as ambassadors and consuls. Ambassadors and consuls represent the United States and keep its interests safe while staying in a foreign nation. They also protect US citizens living in that nation. The secretary of state makes sure all Americans and their belongings are kept safe in foreign countries. They are also

8

responsible for overseeing US immigration policy in other nations. Immigration policy states a nation's rules for foreigners coming into their country to live.

A big part of the secretary of state's job is to work with the leaders of other countries. The secretary of state is in charge of **negotiating** with other nations. For example, the secretary might negotiate with a nation so that a war

Former secretary of state Hillary Clinton meets with Thai children whose homes have been destroyed by floods. As secretary of state, the well-being of children in every country is important.

can be avoided. He or she works with other nations on treaties, which are agreements between countries. The secretary may also break treaties if the other nation does not hold up its part of the agreement. By working with

We rely on the secretary of state to give important speeches. This is how we stay informed about current events in our country and the rest of the world.

other countries, the secretary of state helps to keep peace and grow trade. He or she might choose when to step in when other countries are being unfair to their own citizens. The secretary may help out with humanitarian issues. Humanitarian issues are concerned with human rights to basic needs such as food, shelter, and safety.

The secretary of state also informs, or tells, US citizens about world news. The secretary might make a speech that shares information about the state of relations with another nation. For example, if there is **tension** brewing between the United States and another country, the secretary of state will keep Americans updated. The secretary of state may inform Americans about the **political** and humanitarian issues in foreign nations.

The secretary of state's number one responsibility is to make the best choices for the United States when it comes to foreign relations. He or she tries to help other countries, while also protecting US citizens.

Whom Does the Secretary of State Serve?

The secretary of state is part of the president's cabinet, so he or she serves the president. The secretary also serves citizens by trying to keep peace between nations and protect the human rights of all people!

Secretary of State John Kerry gets ready to board a plane in South Korea during his tour of Asia in February 2014.

CHAPTER TWO

A Day as the Secretary of State

The secretary of state spends a lot of time meeting with world leaders and attending important events. This means he or she spends a lot of time traveling. In fact, Secretary of State John Kerry traveled nearly 280,000 miles (450,616 kilometers) in 2013 alone! Every day is different for the secretary of state because he or she is always in a different place, meeting with new people.

MORNING

A secretary of state's morning starts early! The first meetings or events might start around 8 a.m. If the secretary of state is in the United States, he or she might welcome world

13

Diplomatic meetings help countries talk through their problems and concerns, and create peace.

leaders to our country and host a diplomatic meeting. The secretary of state often meets with ambassadors from other countries. For example, the secretary might meet with the Egyptian ambassador to the United States. They are both

Walking in the Secretary of State's Shoes

William H. Seward was the first secretary of state to travel outside the United States as part of his job. In 1866, Seward traveled to the Caribbean to meet with leaders in the Dominican Republic, Haiti, Cuba, and the Virgin Islands.

representatives who can communicate, or talk about, what's important to their country.

If the secretary is traveling, other world leaders will welcome him or her. Meetings usually last less than an hour before another one starts!

AFTERNOON

The secretary of state might have meetings all day. Other times, they might have to speak at certain events. These events may involve celebrating a certain **culture** or facing issues in a struggling nation. People from the press often cover these events.

Press coverage is when reporters talk about an event on their TV show. Some write about it in newspapers or post it on websites. They might record video or take pictures. This brings attention to the event and gives a public voice to the secretary of state. The press covers the secretary of state's events because it is their job to keep people up to date with foreign relations.

Walking in the Secretary of State's Shoes

The US Department of State holds a press briefing every weekday. This press briefing tells the public about the state of relations with certain countries. It updates people on news about countries with fighting or humanitarian issues.

EVENING

The secretary of state spends a lot of time meeting people. He or she creates good relationships with them. This helps our country stay in a good relationship with other countries. Because of that, the secretary might attend a special event with US leaders, world leaders, and important people in politics and business. These events might include a dinner or reception to honor or welcome a certain person or country.

The secretary of state might also use the evening to travel. Sometimes there are meetings scheduled for the next day in another country. There are many countries to visit and the morning's meetings will start early!

Former secretary of state Condoleeza Rice traveled over 1 million miles (1.6 mil km) when she was secretary of state. Her days were very busy!

WORKING HARD

Every day as the secretary of state is different. He or she may spend the day or night traveling all the way across the world! If you are curious about the kind of work the secretary is doing on any day, the schedule is online at state.gov/r/pa/prs/appt. With meetings, events, and traveling, the secretary of state is always working hard!

Walking in the Secretary of State's Shoes

When the secretary of state travels, many countries are visited in one trip. In November 2014, Secretary of State John Kerry traveled 28,416 miles (45,731 km) in only nine days!

17

President Barack Obama appointed John Kerry as secretary of state during his second term as president.

CHAPTER THREE

Landing the Job

The secretary of state gets to meet almost every important world leader and travel all over the world. He or she is one of the president's top advisors and holds a lot of power. It's a very important job. How does someone land the job of US secretary of state?

There are no specific **requirements** for being the secretary of state. However, the president **appoints** the secretary of state, so that person needs to catch the eye of the president. To be a part of the president's cabinet, a person needs to have the right political ideas, education, and experience to impress the president. The president

This picture shows Hillary Clinton as she is sworn in as US secretary of state in 2009.

carefully chooses the best people for the cabinet, which includes the heads of fifteen departments. Since the secretary of state is the top-appointed official in this cabinet, it is important that he or she stands out to the president!

After the president appoints the secretary of state, that person will need to be approved by the US Senate. The Senate is part of the legislative branch of our government. Members of the Senate represent the interests of their state. This means that a state's voice can be heard in the national, or federal, government. Once the Senate decides that the president has made a good choice, they approve the secretary of state.

There is no specific amount of time a secretary of state has to serve in the position. However, it's usually around four years. That's because the secretary of state works for the president, who serves a four-year term. Once the president leaves, the new president appoints a new secretary

Colin Powell's years of experience in the US military helped him land the job of secretary of state.

of state. The secretary of state may also leave the job on his or her own. A new secretary of state will then be appointed.

What can someone do to become the president's top choice for secretary of state? The president's choice for secretary of state will probably share the beliefs and values of the president. The candidate might have a degree in law or politics. He or she might have experience in politics, whether as a governor, state senator, or leader of a government department. The candidate might also have a lot of experience with foreign relations. This experience might be gained either by serving in the military overseas or working on diplomacy with other countries.

What experiences does a secretary of state need? Condoleezza Rice, who served from 2005 to 2009, earned her PhD in political science and served as President George W. Bush's national security advisor. Hilary Clinton graduated law school, was the first lady, and served as a US senator. Colin Powell served for thirty-five years in the US Army and served as President Ronald Reagan's national security advisor. The careers of these former secretaries of state show that education, government positions, and military service are important for landing the job!

Secretary of State John Kerry

President Barack Obama appointed John Kerry as secretary of state in 2013 based on his excellent career. Kerry graduated from Yale University, served in the US Navy, and was a US senator. He also served as lieutenant governor of Massachusetts and chairman of the Senate Foreign Relations Committee. He tackled many important issues, including services for returned soldiers and humanitarian issues all over the world.

Computers and books are great places to look for information about our government.

CHAPTER FOUR

Getting Involved in Government!

Do you like to travel? Are you interested in making peace between different countries and standing up for humanitarian issues? Does a job as the secretary of state sound like the right job for you?

Many states have their own secretary of state, but there's only one US secretary of state in the whole country. That means this position is a hard one to come by. However, the best way to work toward this goal is by getting involved in government and international relations.

You can research the different branches of government and the different departments. What do these

Every city has its own city hall. Each structure holds many important departmental offices and meeting rooms for local politicians.

branches and departments do? You can also learn hands-on about government by getting involved in your local government. Visit your local city hall, or attend a city council meeting. This is where many important community issues are talked about. You can also write letters to local politicians about issues in your community. When you're old enough, you can vote for politicians who will run the country, state, or city in the best way possible.

A good secretary of state knows a lot about different cultures and world issues. You can start your research now! Learn about countries around the world. Read world

There are many rich cultures to discover around the world. Dance, food, language, and other ways of life make up a person's culture.

news reports or tune in to news programs. This will keep you updated on world events. Which countries need our help? Which countries have humanitarian issues, such as **poverty**? Learn about different holidays, customs, and foods from other countries, too. The secretary of state works very hard to **relate** to people from around the world, so learning about different cultures is important.

Your school may have a student government with class leaders, such as presidents and secretaries. Take on a leadership position. This is a great way to learn about how

Making friends with people who are different from you is a great way to learn new things and open your mind.

democracy works. You can also reach out to people in your school or community who have just moved to our country. Introduce yourself. Ask them about their experiences. Always be friendly to others and open to learn about other cultures. Just like the secretary of state, you can build friendships with people from all around the world!

Get Involved!

Volunteering is a great way to meet new people, learn about your community, and find out about important issues. A great volunteer organization is Key Club. Key Club allows students to perform volunteer service, develop leadership skills, and become good citizens!

advise To help someone else make a decision.

appoint To choose someone for a job.

citizen A member of a country.

culture The ways or practices of a group of people.

democracy A government in which people have power through representatives they elect.

foreign Having to do with a country that is not one's own; outside a place or country.

negotiate To try to come to an agreement with a person or group.

official A person who holds an office in government.

political Having to do with the activities or practices of leaders in government.

poverty The condition of being very poor.

relate To have a connection with something or someone.

relationship A connection of some kind.

representative A person who speaks or acts for a group of people.

requirement Something that you must do or have.

tension Negative feelings between people or groups.

FIND OUT MORE!

BOOKS

Landau, Elaine. *Searchlight Books: The President, Vice President, and Cabinet: A Look at the Executive Branch.* Minneapolis, MN: Lerner Publications, 2012.

Rajczak, Michael. *Meet the President's Cabinet.* New York: Gareth Stevens Publishing, 2013.

Ruffin, David C. *The Duties and Responsibilities of the Secretary of State*. New York: PowerKids Press, 2005.

WEBSITES

Ben's Guide: The President's Cabinet
bensguide.gpo.gov/3-5/government/national/cabinet.html

Government for Kids: Three Branches of Government
kids.usa.gov/three-branches-of-government

Travels with Secretary Kerry
www.state.gov/secretary/travel/index.htm

MEET THE AUTHOR

Caitie McAneney is an author and editor from Buffalo, New York. She has written many books for young readers. She enjoys drinking hot tea, reading old books, and hanging out with her cat, Big Tuna.

INDEX

Page numbers in **boldface** are illustrations.